The
Memory
Orchard

The
Memory
Orchard

Tim Bowling

Brick Books

National Library of Canada Cataloguing in Publication

Bowling, Tim, 1964-
    The memory orchard / Tim Bowling

Poems.
ISBN 1-894078-34-9

    I. Title.

PS8553.O9044M45 2004   C811'.54   C2003-907223-1

We acknowledge the support of the Canada Council for the Arts, the
Government of Canada through the Book Publishing Industry
Development Program (BPIDP), and the Ontario Arts Council for
their support of our publishing program.

The cover is after a photograph by Maureen Scott Harris.

The book is set in Minion and Galliard.

Design and layout by Alan Siu.

Printed and bound by Sunville Printco Inc.

Brick Books
431 Boler Road, Box 20081
London, Ontario N6K 4G6

brick.books@sympatico.ca

for
Russell Thornton

CONTENTS

The Call   11

I

The Memory Orchard   15
Where the River Meets the Ocean   17
Tsawwassen 1968, Toronto 1931   19
Memory   20
Mannequins   22
The String   25
Adolescence   27
Does the World Remember Us?   29
September   31
Message to the World   32

II

Late for the Doubleheader, 1970   35
Widow   36
Pennies on the Sidewalk   39
Brothers   41
Old Trucks   42
Technology   43
November   44
The Great War   45
Dead Whale on the Ferry Causeway   46
April   47
Insomnia   48
Medieval   49
Snowfall   50

III

Two Tourists 55
Stonehenge 57
Paris, Youth, Springtime 59
Dead Man in the Badlands 61
Watching the Academy Awards in the Bar
    of the Patricia Hotel 63
Earth 64
Owl Pellet 65

IV

Grade One 69
Preparing to Write 70
How to Live the Examined Life 72
Ladders 74
Poets 75
For Edward Thomas and David O'Meara 76
Classic 77

V

Conception 81
Young Men Fall in Love With Their Misery,
    Those Older Know It's Cold 82
Trainyards 83
For Your Birthday 84
Argument 86
Rain on Sunday Afternoon 88

The Stern-End 93

Acknowledgements 97
Biography 99

The Call

In the high windstorms of the coast
the power is always going out
like the voice of God in our time.
Children are sent for candles
or if there are no children
the grown search in drawers alone.
Now the rain down the windowpanes
and the wax down the candles
and the tears down the face
make their almost-silent trinity.

The phone rings, and the voice
of my childhood says
The power is out.
I'm sitting here in the dark.

And the words
travelling such a long way
charge the air: there's a sheen
around my hand
the colour of wet cedar
and a sudden breath of river
the tide running down.

What do we say to our pasts
as we grow older
that will not betray them
with lies, betray them
with truth?

I can think of nothing
and the voice, quieter,
as if talking to itself,
keeps on:

Are you there? Are you listening?
I'm getting cold. Can you hear the rain?

The Memory Orchard

It was planted by the dead
to keep each human system of nerves
vital, involved, complicated. If
the flesh could not go on holding us,
at least these branches would.
Springs, we lulled there, cradled.
Winters, though we couldn't name it,
we felt the thrill of the bared sinews
of the upthrust arm of God.
Pear or apple, cherry or plum —
the house it belonged to,
that sigh-softened wood,
was gone, only the rotted plank
of a root-cellar lid in the tall grass,
and English voices still teased
like taffy on the wind, remained.

All body, we crossed to the trees.
All spirit, we hung there, ripening
with the fruit around us, ripening
like the stars at night.

The town is done with orchards now.
All were levelled decades past.
Children no longer climb
among the petticoats and kisses
and the dim lanterns
of the pears' flesh
lighting the salmon's journey home.
Mothers' voices do not tangle
in the fretwork
of first solitude.

Yet one alone remains,
rain-battered decks and scaffolds
of love, touch without presence,
speech without words,

the style of our ascension:
our faces aging where the fruit was,
we look around, bewildered,
awed, root and branch,
reluctant windfall,
edging over a little
on the frost in the air,
making room
for fresh blood in the barrel.

Where the River Meets the Ocean

for Theresa Shea

Many old barns and families
of bats asleep in the beams.
An all-day rain. Drops
off the poplars, slow depending,
embryonic, translucent bats.
The downward weight of life
like the carp in the tide
that have swallowed the hooks
the boys left to dangle
off the wharf,
like the bloodcaked workshirts
of the slaughterhouse men
changing to dark glistens
on the landlady's clothesline.

Towards dusk
a cat gives birth
to fifteen kittens
all but three of which
the owls will kill
before dawn:
those tiny, hungering mouths
descend as we did
along the dark canal
one of the three alive
on a planet of death
as mere fathoms off
in the world of salt
the newborn hangs
pendulous
from the mother whale
and rolls away
like a tear the earth would cry
if it could feel as we feel.

How do we feel?

The skinny arms
of two headlights
search for their gloves
among the cattails
along each side
of the river road
(the gloves hanging neatly,
hidden in the barns).
The land runs out on the search
as Time runs out on us.

Dark soon. The stars open
every crevice in the wood
(as her love does my will).
Home is always love and pain,
touching and leaving the earth
as if it were a body.

And so we are here.
And here is how we feel.

Tsawwassen 1968, Toronto 1931

The rotting whale, the rental house.
Wakened, I was taken to see the sea
monster, under stars. It stank.
I cried in the brine tears of brine.
No one ever took me
to our wood's decay.

And so I go.
The rental house, the rotting whale,
the tongue's swung gate, the door's rust creak,
I enter by, corsage of gills
at my lapel, to better breathe
my boyhood's and my bloodcells' stink.
The rental house, the rotting whale,
steps in the blubber, sperm on the walls.
Grandmother in your flesh-kitchen, calving
babies for the earth's embrace, Grandfather
at the gaping closet of the night
with nothing to wear for your vanished work:
will you pour for my travels a candle of oil
to scorch the mildew off the dark?

The rotting house, the whale I rent,
the tattered paper of the boneways,
I turn at the door, I turn at, I turn,
the cracked eye of the ocean
the bloodshot window of the slum
eighty years of the bagged salt of grief
on my shoulders, I stagger and reach
for hands I never held in life,
and shiver to touch the brine in the bone.

Memory

I write this with the hot ink
of the red stripe on the back
of a garter snake stopped
a second in the tall grass
beside the Fraser River
under a sky of August fire.

I reached into a closet
racked with bones
in a condemned house
I put my arm through
the dark of the dead
to wet this quill
I leaned all my weight
on the dust and air
(nobody there
but this moment, still.)

My younger arm
I kept behind, the one
that stayed six seconds
longer in the womb.
With the other
like a blind man's
cane, heavy
with all weather,
I went back
and dipped
my right index finger
into the baked
strip of flesh
parallel to, still
as, the river.

I did not touch
the child who stood
just as still
beside the snake
though his hand
was hot and open
at his side
and full of blood.

Here is the poem
of the low red smoke
in the permanent
grass. I want
you to read this
as the child read
that stillness
of the world,

quickly
with the older
and then, slowing,

      the younger eye.

Mannequins

Some canny developer bought
a whole town-block of shops
and shut them down and
let their insides die. Rainy
afternoons, we stepped lightly
through the long-smashed panes
of streetfront glass and found
eternal dusk, the ring
of a mortal register echoing
like a stone dropped
farther and farther down
a well until all we could hear
is what memory hears,
bolts of fabric measured out
in the supple, cadenced tones
our parents' parents
lovingly applied
to the shadows of the living ear.

It was in the dress shop
that we moved among
the standing figures
whose naked, thickened torsos
cast a moon's light
on the shards and dust.
Maternal, but only for
the spaces where we'd been,
the ladies had the headless
heft of tombs and
wrapped their armless love
around the us that wasn't
us, not yet, just as the names
on tombstones spell our names
in different letters.

Day by day, the dress shop
swirled its filmic dust
until it seemed we'd floated up
to the light between
the image and the turning reel
and breathed there,
amber-caught,
while the ladies had come
halfway from a silent short
to join us.

But for what purpose,
we couldn't say. I still
can't say.

Except, at times,
my children reading
by the rain-streaked glass,
or the August sun setting
on marshes of salt
where the pewter fish sign
their covenant with rust,
I feel the heavy,
camphored breasts
press against the self
my boyhood housed
who now peeks out
a little more intensely
each hour of each day
as if my eyes were windows
of a shop
where vigilant, caring women
and gently looting children
listen together

to the dark brother of the dust
as it falls and pools
on the cracked sidewalk
while the heart, because
it is always where it was
and where it is going,
gives firmly back the rhythm
of the stillness in the human stone.

The String

A gentle tug would wake me in the fish-rich dawn,
my almost-attic sleep disturbed by plan,
the net twine looped around and knotted
to my wrist, the far end
lifted from the dewed grass and cedar
sawdust underneath my bedroom window
by my boyhood's first, best, destined-not-
to-last friendship, of the rust-haired,
freckled fisherman's son whose own sleep
lay in proportion to the moon
as the blood in the gull to its feathers.

And I would turn, blinking,
to the grey light and the hard press
of the shovel's blade in my instep arch
and the fat worms clustered in the steaming
compost pile and skinny lines
plunked into muddy currents,
but first, that subtle pressure
on my wrist that spread slowly
through my body till I rose and
crossed the peeled linoleum
and, looking down, found
the daybreak's human parallel,
a reflection clearer than
its source, a blood-awaking grin,
and the immaculate unnecessity of voice.

Where once my senses fused and rushed
into the day's artful lack of artifice
quietly down the ghost-kept stairs
into the breaking surf of dogwood blossom,
now the rare, faint tug engenders speech
more like the ugly, gaping fish
we left to leach their oils on the wharf
than any urgent call to wonder, cry to praise.
Where once I rose and went

to kneel without prayer, I rise
seeking the true word for living,
but find only the wash of rain
filling the boys' naked prints,
and brown stains on the blossoms,
rust on the hinges of change,
splintered hardwood on the descent to the world.

Who holds the unseen string, who
anticipates a drowsy presence at a window
smeared with morning, and stands,
vine-still, in a brazier
of sawdust? There's no one there.
Neither child nor man.

Yet I pray the soul be taken from us
with the ease of being
on the wrist, that doesn't say
"It's time," or even "Come,"
but, soundless as the dawn
removes the stars, as a boy
pulls what he loves and what he kills
towards him, grinning,
leads us to the light impress
of what we were, all we are,
a faint passage along a muddy bank
through the fraying edges of the day
into the taut horizon and the grave-grass snarl.

Adolescence

Spiderwebs thick as smoke in the blackberries,
and the fruit overripe, falling soot,
whole bushes trembling like steam engines
in vacant lots, the town's old sidings
where fishermen's whelped have knifed their names
in dying orchards, the trunks
tough as eagle claw, black as char.

And across the flats the real rail-line
is rarely used, dangles in the rain
like a rope-ladder down
a shrouded cliff. Between
the coalcars and the blackberries
is nothing and everything: my life.

I mean where the world came in
the smell and sound and taste
how the gulls were several shades of grey
but sometimes such a vivid white
you almost blinked for pain. I mean
the grass where you learned the word
for grass, and how you imagined the dead
waving the fronds of their arms
as they rushed by you in your sleep.
I mean your life, any past.

Half the schoolyard in broken beer bottles
and the other half in frost. A girl
named Violet with a weed for a mouth.
The silent coupling of the mangy dogs
you watched and could not breathe
your breath. Trying to read an invitation
in the guarded cadence of her laugh.

There was a spirit behind that look
the world tried to kill, a fresh-caught
genie in the bottle of the flesh.
But if you looked out on ugliness

you saw it only as a partial truth
and bid the blood to swell its banks.

No one takes from us what we
don't partly give. I am keeping back
the squished black of the fruit
so the world can't blend it
to a headline. The smashed
glass drunken with winter sun
reflects only the natal thrusts
of shadow and light.

The gulls peel off the blue mountains there,
loose birchbark carved with the names
and dates of the child's hour,
mine and yours. We were beautiful
in longing once, and –
murmurous engines of our life
in the smoke, engaged – we are.

Does the World Remember Us?

Sated with garbage and guts
the gulls on the roof-peak
saw me lick the scent of black-
berry from her bronzing shoulder
and gawked as, storm-browed,
I pelted stray cats with rocks.
When weren't they there,
those brine-eyed judges
in their robes of ash, turning
into the wind to watch me puke
my first cheap bottle, stretching
their necks toward the time
I helped the mind-blank
and shivering old neighbour home.

And how many pitiable bullheads
gaped in terror at my blue intention
to destroy, or dew-fleshed salmon
saw my hand-tombs scrape across
their vision of the infinite and clear?

It must be coded in the species now,
so that this very moment's
gulls and fish must sometimes snap
awake to flashes of remoter terror
so real they seem less like the present
than the past the long dead
of their own kind lived
(where even acts of gentleness
fade in the quick of killing).

Memory keeps the suffering vigilant.

From the rooftops, the deep tides,
out of ditchbanks, cloud-currents,
telephone wires, prickle bushes,
beyond compost piles, shed-shadows,

wharf-shadows, grass-shadows —
this flinch from the imprint of power.

Senses wide, I remember
the world's gallied look
and a weeping so quiet
those years couldn't hear it
for the sound of moths
shaking the dark off their wings.

September

One ripe blackberry left on the bush,
one spider in a web of all the broken strands
of every spider's life, the left side of the salmon's
face, the side that didn't see its death.

Dark burl in the coffin,
harpoon-wound in the day-flesh,
one child's morning of ink
whorled into the truant's globe.

Starlight plunges into it, and river-flow.
It swells slightly
when the old woman on her deathbed
remembers how she'd pricked
her finger as a newlywed
sewing her husband's shirts,
and swells when the baby bruises
his lips on language.

Quarried out of the earth
by birdsong and rain. Small
volcano blackened by lava-spill.
It has outlived its age,
hanging in its Elizabethan collar,
waiting for the guards to come.

Hold it in your palm.
For a second, you can live
in the senses of the past again
before the summer is gone
and the gulls take up forever
the raucous occasions of Time.

Message to the World

Any letters for me, please put them
in the burnt-out jack-o'-lantern.
If you find a fallen leaf
from my tenth or thirtieth year
please hang it on the clothesline
with my grandmother's linen.
Please don't press your face
to the screen on the porch door;
the moth-hunger in the human eye
is more than I can bear.
Tomorrow, perhaps, I'll begin again
the terrifying life of heart and muscle,
scrape the ash from the lantern
and circle my eyes, reel in the damp
of memory on its rusty wheel,
and greet you as any other man.
But not tonight. Please,
if you would come to me at all,
come as the smoke of one fire
to another, or as the voice of the moon
to the body of the slackened river.

Late for the Doubleheader, 1970

My older brother's hair hung long and ragged as a crow's wing.
He climbed the hundred-foot fir tree in the vacant lot
in his powder blue, striped Ladner Fishermen fastball uniform
until eventually I couldn't see his cleats against the sun.

He climbed out of the goodness of his heart
(our mother would have said, our grandmother)
to rescue a starling that had somehow snagged
itself on a piece of net twine and dangled
off a bough, swinging like a burning censer
in the wind. It cried and cried.
The tomcats shook like kids under a pinata.

I stood by the trunk, squinting. My brother,
the dark angel in pastels, disappeared, lost
as one of Franklin's men in the rigging.
He climbed out of the goodness of his heart
and left me down here with the years
and the tiny black shadow of the starling
searching over the burnt grass like a hand
on the bedcovers for a pack of smokes
in the dark for another hand, for love.

My brother always climbs out of his heart.
But it's the starling's shadow I wear
in the world, and cry, though my hand
that summer day reached out and found
the blood of my kind in the glove.

Widow

City girl, what have you done,
up to your elbows in ducks' blood
and salmon guts, the black smear
of the coal cars across the mudflats
your only lipstick: here,
where the salt marsh gladly
gathers the eyes' brine to its rushes
for the songbirds to sip
and add the faraway to the windowsill's melody?

City girl, where have you gone,
who once clutched a ticket
for the trolley-car and journeyed
from your parents' grubby rented parlour,
under the cracked eyes
of the Queen Street madhouse
where an inmate axed
your uncle's skull in half
(you shuddered at the phantom
laughter every trip),
to the dance where the fighting men
of many nations fought
for the chance to jitterbug with you,
so poor you could not afford the paint
to fake black seams of stockings
on your legs, so innocent
you believed the factory girls
who told you a prophylactic
was a casing for the butcher's sausage,
o city girl, what did you feel
when you missed your stop
and the trolley reached the end
of the line, and the driver was gone,
the windows smashed, and the chill
wind off an ocean you never imagined
tore the brotherly kiss of the Scottish pilot
from your cheek and the ticket from

your hand, and you stepped off
in bridal white, married to cuteness
and gentle blue eyes, four babies
who lived, one leaden at his cord,
fifty-six years of doing, always doing,
at your heart's dictates, for others,
even to the gutting of the winged,
until your child's voice woke you to say
"He's gone," and now you daily
sink a crimson rose in tepid water
beside an urn of ashes?

Child of poverty, my dear remainder,
rare survivor of the century's plagues,
eight siblings lost before your birth,
with what sorrow do you tell
how the midwife came in one door
while the undertaker went out the other,
how your mother begged for you to stay
(her baby, her last) just one week more,
then turned to a granite slab in her bed
as you grew used to sharing yours?

Little lost one, Depression waif,
the gulls fly up for me like tickets
from the blood of the river. If
I could reach them and hold them
and board what is left of your life,
where could I be taken
that holds more beauty and truth
than into the long memory of you
at the sink, red-wristed, sweating,
your hands soaked with the viscera
of living, plunged into the thick
of your own heart's pounding,
where could I go, my almost orphan,
more desolate and broken

than into the saying of the words
that wake the survivor of a love
to clean rooms, long naps,
windows open onto salt
and the blood of the past ebbing slowly in the pipes?

Pennies on the Sidewalk

The dead, for all we know,
wear little German shoes and
leave us frozen crumbs, because
the forest is dark even at midday
and weird shadows sidle fleshed
over the pine-needled floor. And since
the dead aren't coming back to us,
we must look out for them, though
the trail is widely scattered and will
take us all our lives to track, a crumb
here, a crumb there, different cities,
countries, continents, the real-estate
holdings of the dead more vast
than those of the Catholic Church.

Just this morning I found the last
brass button off the greatcoat worn
in the trenches of the Somme
by the sole surviving soldier of that war,
and, wiping off the blood, I saw
his King and heard his oath,
then watched the death of faith
invade his eyes, and understood
the horror in the midwife's stare
as she held the future's irony
in her slippery hands. So much mud,
we might never wash it off.

Yet I also found, three weeks before,
a rusted tear my mother cried
because the red-winged blackbirds
at her feeder sang a soft Italian air
out of her threadbare urban childhood,
and she was briefly sad with happiness
at the lucent window of the world.

We are all followers in the dark wood
and the way is lit only by small tokens —

a few words, a date, the picture of a Queen.

When we walk over them,
the air trembles a little,
and night falls
when it falls
like dirt off the sides of an open grave.

Brothers

One's rattling crates of liquor
down nightclub and restaurant chutes
in Greater Vancouver,
one's clanging a wrench
against the pipes of a BC ferry,
one's dead, the stranger
who came blue and twisted
from the womb, and gave me
the chance to live. Brother,
and I speak to you all,
cease for a moment your labour,
as I will cease my inessential
own. Breathe one rhythm with me
in the middle of your day
before our work is done and,
ghosts, we begin again together.

Old Trucks

Suddenly, almost anywhere, my grandfather's tomb.
And often, in the wheel wells, wildflowers,
or, thrown across the dusty windshield, a honey-
suckle vine, blackberry bramble, like
Mary Pickford's arm across her brow.

I stand bare-headed, a phantom
fedora kneaded in my hands,
a phantom handkerchief
the size of a tablecloth folded
in my pocket where the railway watch
shivers down soot with every second.

The wind is always the wind of the breadline.
The fields are always black and white.
The passenger side is always empty.

If I ever moved closer, I might find
in the backseat a newspaper column
friendly to labour, or on the dash
some horehound candy speckled with lint.
I might put my heart to the wheel
and steer for the constellations.

But no. I buy my gasoline from strangers
and get where I'm going much faster.
Mostly, I don't stop for tombs.
Somehow, always, there are fewer.

The wildflowers wilt. Rust advances
a foot in its war of attrition.
The girl faints again in silent horror.

Technology

In the middle of a city,
a roadside church, the nearby
traffic-light on red. Suddenly
the bells begin to chime.
I am called to the medieval sphere
the Great Chain of Being
the Sioux circle, the Great Spirit,
the million perfect moons
on the body of the salmon
the silver ring of the wake
of the last leap before death
the sun's slashed eye on the bison's crash
to the bottom of the jump,
I am called by what
a human hunger needed
once, and almost go,
the spire of cedar smoke
above the river, sage smoke
blowing over the plains,
but the light changes
and the gunned engines drown
the bells, as the ocean
drowns the heartbeat of the whale,
until the road is empty
and the air still, and all
my compulsions to complete
this sudden longing in a circle
are torn by the world
as if swarms of flies
had found, one chill dawn,
no spun cathedrals
to limit their ravening
at the lips of the dead.

November

What is the weather doing tonight
to the names of the three brothers
chiselled in the cenotaph's granite
in the little park at the centre
of Sackville, New Brunswick?

Rain, be kind to them.
Sun, be kinder.

To Arlington, Joseph, and George.

Be no accomplice to memory,

the most delicate murderer.

The Great War

My fathers were the honey men
housing live swarms in basements
through Edmonton winters
in the golden years
before the single bee buzzed the Archduke's throat.

They pedalled heavy bicycles
over rough roads
and cried "Fresh from the combs!"
who'd later crack blood-engorged lice
between thumb and forefinger, down in the trenches,
in spring, with neither wine nor honey
to pay passage to the world of the dead.

My mothers were all alone on the earth
with the occasional drone
stirring below among the empty boxes
and helmets of mesh, then crawling
a few inches to die on the stone.

I was left with the shrapnel of summer,
each bee blood-dipped
and swarming tight
to make a pomegranate: one taste
and I was destined to spend
(like everyone else)
half my life in the memory
of who my people might have been.

Dead Whale on the Ferry Causeway

Your only mourners are the stars.
They arrive slowly, stay all night.

At daybreak
a gull walks between
the empty beer bottles
the teenagers arranged
like birthday candles
on your bulk,
then flies off,
a vivid flare.

But there's no rescue now.

The absence of god
is filled with the longing
for the presence of god.

Night after night,
the stars attend
your stench
as scholars attend
the turning of time
into history.

April

Lilac bushes bulk the dusk
at the sides of sagging porches.
Beached whales, they sounded
the molten core while we slept
and rose to speak of it
in gasping essences.

A light, translucent rain
makes them shiver with fear
and sweeten their musk protectively
as darkness deepens. Soon,
they will be black in the blackness
as the newly-dug grave
in the middle of the first night
of grief, as the ash of the fire
between the stars and bats' bodies
long after the fire has gone out.

All night, this gloved, velvet
weight on our skin
where we sleep
by glassless spaces.

Then the old women at daybreak
flensing strips from the wondrous
to have always at the throat
as they drift through dusted rooms
of cloying lemon
a wet hand from the sea
and, at the ear, a salt voice
sounding out of great depths
with insistent tenderness: "Wake."

Insomnia

The turned and watered earth
of the flower beds that moat
our sinking, sagging bungalow
is sea-cold and dark
as starlessness.
Its black collars
my heart's unease,
ribs gripping the terrified hare.
I should be soothed
by so much life thrusting
to the surface, except
I sense the bulbs only
as the thief on the scaffold
senses the gawking mob.

Who can rest from hunger
in a world that's never sated?

I lie at the angle of the worms,
breathing slowly, holding still
in the middle space, while
tiny hammers all around me
beat into shape
the impossible pewter nave of no-God.

Medieval

Through the doorway window-glass
I thought I saw Death in the street
out seeking an address
but it was only the hooded neighbour boy,
shovel hoisted to his shoulder,
off to lift the snowfall
from his parents' walk.

I counted three quick heartbeats:
for my father, my brother, and
the girlhood of the woman I love –
then let them go to the dark,
terrified sparrows alone
over the owl's-head earth.

Behind me,
in the house and history,
the clock ticked like a mother's scolding.
Time always wants us to be careful;
that's why we created it. Okay, Mom,
I'll call my heartbeats home.

Then
when the black shape rings the bell
I can greet through snowflakes
(my self entire with its losses)
the unallowanced grin of bone.

Snowfall

Busy sexton of the footstep's grave
you will not rest
until every trace
of the blood-borne is gone,
you, the most serious weather,
because you contrast greater
with night and bare branches
and the hollows under the eyes,
because, with your lamb's colour,
your ephemerality is sadder
than the rain's.

Anyone can walk out of you
and appear mysterious, but no one's
coming will survive. How quietly
you give yourself to rivers,
streets, the tongues of children —
is it death you are trying to teach us?

Funny how you've always been:
falling as the dinosaurs clashed in
the swamps, catching the rag-clad
prostitute's eye as she blinked
up at the gas-lamps, settling
over the landfills filled
with dial phones and last year's
terminals, their screens
space-black forever. We want
fire and loved ones when
you're here, we prefer arrivals
to departures. Gentle graveman,
you tell us that we will have to go
from this world at last, but tell us
as a mother explains
the concept of dying to her child,
with the sad love of truth.

Being silent, being serious,
you warm the black combs
of the riddled hive of the earth.

Two Tourists

And went into the cathedral at Wells,
unchilded, new to each other, first maps on the skin.
Among the English long dead, English drear living,
in violent windbreakers of our young country's coast
went stone to stone reading, hand-holding,
mouthing the Latin griefs, feeling the chill
that is the shadow of the inside of the shadow
that is History, wearing the fine island mist
on our brows, and behind it, behind our thinking,
the faintest carolling of sheeps' bells as the flocks
of the centuries leave their fleece on the hills
and the crooks lean in stone corners unused,
and whispered "evensong" in the late afternoon,
dreaming of a boys' choir rinsing the air
with octaves, who didn't know evensong
or any ritual, just longed for whatever
gilt flight in the throat had built
this hard bone for the body of Heaven,
and followed three monks in cassocks
where they stepped out of a doorway, heads
hooded bowed, and not even monks
in cassocks, not even a doorway, but lacked
even the words for evensong, thinking
only to be lifted from the harshness, briefly,
of the soft English earth and sad English eyes
into what the newness of each other was,
spring in a scribed manuscript, "showres soote,"
until reached the sparse congregation
of elderly locals and heard the priest's
voice, not a priest's voice, intone
without music words whose meaning
was the gravity of age, words like stone
over which the tongue was moss,
and blushed at the weight of the cameras
round our necks, and the giddiness
of love in a foreign place as the voice
sought our prayers for the sister

with cancer may God hold her
in the hollow of His hand and
had a kind parishioner in the pew
beside instruct us how to kneel
and dumbshow faith for half an hour
in the beautiful last light of England
under the scaffolding of restoration
near where the Romans took the waters
clutching our cold pence for the plate
while rain touched the glass brow of Mary
and the bared heels of the infant Christ
and heard each other softly breathing
and the blood in our veins slowed
as if for cygnets and recited psalms
and went out of the cathedral at Wells
into the blurred green and last birdcall
shrouded in dusk for the journey.

Stonehenge

A hall of mirrors
giving back the one
altered expression.

We can't move quickly
around this stone
but take steps
small as those
who brought it here.

There is the path of the body
and the path of the mind
and the path of the spirit

and they all trail off
into space, the darkness
between these pillars
the darkness between stars
between waking and sleep.

At seventeen,
with the English canon
on my desk, I thought
I understood for a few
fleeting seconds
negative capability
as the feeling of an emotion
so powerfully
it became its opposite.

I don't know if that's true,
but under this English sky
silence turns to a scream
and the hung jaws
in the mirrors
float yoked and separate
to the terror,

everything trembling
the way the clear waters
of a salmon creek
explode at leaf-fall
and even the idling
Japanese tour buses
excite the scale.

Paris, Youth, Springtime

Someone somewhere in the grey web of streets
was having an important feeling over absinthe
but I was the fly on the drab strand
staring down the spider's pilots. A dozen
impossible blocks away, over a span
of rooftops murky and uneven as the ocean floor,
the permanent autumn of the oils
in the Louvre broke and broke again
the widening heart of some chiropractor's
daughter from the American midwest,
but I lived the four seasons of home
in a dingy, unromantic garret where
whole centuries of artists no one
ever heard of eked out
their scribbling, dabbing bitternesses.

The City of Lights shivered grey-black
but for the dome of the Sacré Coeur
that floated in the streaked window,
locked in like an aquarium beluga.

Two days of rain, my sister ill,
that whale was my one companion.
He spoke the language of mosses
and cedars, the mutual hunger
for our lost Pacific salt. Two
spiders in every stranger's face
closed in when I walked the streets
in search of take-out food. I came
to see my whale as a fellow victim
sucked by the same cold fangs
to a pallid husk. The guidebooks
cried "Live! Live!" The heart,

on its old streetcar lines
to the private truth, whispered
"Elsewhere."

There are days even now
when the weight of the black Paris rain
breaks a fir branch in my back
and the blood of my young hands
throbs in the ashy breasts
of the pigeons on the Champs Elysées.

If I ever go back,
it will be for my child, that loneliness,
my brother, those wanderings,
and to walk up to the sadness
in the eyes of my great friend who,
unlike the webbed fly
with its desperate chances
and tiny beating heart,
never managed a way out.

Dead Man in the Badlands

At the foot of a sandstone butte
he lies, broken-necked. His flesh
will be picked clean, his bones
will be common to all but
his own kind, who will never
find him. Missing, presumed
dead. Or presumed missing.
After all, men have a knack
for going places that aren't death
until there is nowhere else for them
to go. And it doesn't even matter
why he was here, or why
he fell. His heart has stopped.
Mosquitoes discover no happy glut
in the veins of his throat. He lies
in the matrix of his disappearing name.
His eyes return no light to the stars
which, without sound,
hammer him into the dark.
A whole valley for a grave,
extinction for a grave-mate,
the powder of mule deer and
coyote, the ground lime
of the living that he was
hours before, the lime
he now is to sweeten
a rare crack in the stone
for the birth of a crocus.
The dawn will come
with its warm mouth
again and again
to sup without sustenance
the outer layer from
the final white. It's a form
of love, the one kind
left to him. Under

the vast All, only Time
and his poor skeleton
can make him feel
at home.

Watching the Academy Awards
in the Bar of the Patricia Hotel

A woman somewhere is winning something.
The dark cleave between her roundnesses
parallels the landscape outside
this almost empty place. No. It's no
use. There are no parallels. We're
on another planet. And yet
the giant wooden Albertosaurus
outside the one-pump gas station
selling stale bread and overripe fruit
is pure Hollywood. I can imagine
the toothsome starlet slinkily posed
beside the open jaws, Fay Wray
of the fossil set. No. I can't.
If there are a million shutter whirrs
in the mosquito drone, only
the God of heat and coyote-echo
stands behind that camera.

The victories here are without gloss
and for the self. Someone, this weekend,
might win a bet on the calf-roping
at the circuit rodeo. More likely, though,
the day will be got through minus
all but the heart's most local hurrah.

Here, the stars are real and stone-heavy.
The eyes of the world don't look
out of their high-corner static and blur,
and we only look part way in.
Horses to break, bones to dig,
poems to write. Gentlemen, raise a glass
to the sweat and the ache and the awe
of the work unsung, the life unglamorous.

Earth

The great wings, the continents,
are folded close. It has left
its one white egg unattended.
Nothing has happened for a long time.
The red vest of the hunter approaches
slowly through the dark woods again.

Owl Pellet

This is the only letter God will ever send you.
And if, opening it, you expect answers,
advice, condolences, you will find
a signature of bone. Otherwise,
a great hunched watchfulness
will leave your body, and perch
on the black branch between stars.

Grade One

Out of Miss Robinson's ringless hand, the letters
rose like smoke on the night-black blackboard.
I closed my eyes. Her perfume wafted
through mingled scents of glue and apple-core
until I thought the strange, chalk figures
were a slow smoulder off her skin.

She had the most beautiful auburn hair,
its shade the early rouge on a gravenstein.
Recess-rumour said she once dated Bobby Orr.

The musk of old rain
steamed off our coats and boots
clustered in the cloakroom
where there hung no cloaks.

We sat in our desks as if we had boarded a train
that would take us to knowledge of the clock-face
looming over our clasped hands and clear brows.

Something was ticking down all around us
but it couldn't be the hour. We didn't know hours.

Miss Robinson sighed
as she flamed the entrance to the cave.

Slowly, I opened my eyes on the vowels.

Preparing to Write

I went out and pressed my heart to the earth
as I last did a quarter century past,
and my grave rushed forward as
my boyhood rushed back,
supple mouths of the same bitch
gentle on the scruff of her pups
savage to tear the threatening flesh,
but I could not tell which mouth
fit the grave and which the child
so I hugged the flooding images
in the grass and let them come
as dark comes to the stars,
with an approach that means light.

Soon my heart became again
an anthill for my hungering veins.
I let those red armies march,
bringing what plunder they had found
in over thirty years of searching,
and then I killed the killing metaphors.

The sun found me, as if it remembered
the exact ploughing plunge
of my hipbones, how my jawbone
slid neatly into its envelope of soil.
The wind tucked its mother-blanket in
around my sides, then tore it off —
the old dual game I'd forgotten
the impersonal insistence of.
And the planet whispered once more
in the voice of grating rock
and trickling creek
"I'm as prey to death as you are."

And I felt the lost rising, the soul-whirl,
the field dropping away to become
a flannel pocket to hold my body
as I rose, gull-white, loosed

handkerchief of being. I saw
the long shadows of dusk
step out from the trees and
telephone poles, like cloaked men
covering the earth, seeking
the absenting light, and I knew
my blood was in that motion,
longing for what I alone possessed,
and I descended with pity for
the years that had to come,
the bitch licking and snarling
as I raised my heart
like a cup of rainwater
and returned to the world
spilling a little
for the ache of our continuance.

How to Live the Examined Life

I'm a poor man but I pay to be shaved.
Three times a week, because three
is a magical number (Christ died at double
three, and Hart Crane jumped ship). The days
in between, I wear my face's dark
as if God's graphite pencil had shaded
my heart's every nuance for the world
to see. "Look," the people point, "adult sorrow."
And then Nick the barber shaves me clean
to smile with joy at children again.

Nick speaks little English (he's Lebanese),
just croons foreignly with the blade
at my throat, tipping it gently
so that I think he might be
gleaning a drop of water from a petal.
And how conscious I am of my blood
beneath the surface, and of my
amazingly vulnerable Adam's apple
out there alone, breathing like a sparrow.
"Close?" Nick says as always. "Yes,
close," I reply as always, then
relax my muscles and shut my eyes
and let the hands black with
fine hairs scrape the ashes
until I rise, a craterless moon,
to shine three days a week
(a decent record for any man)
on the prophets and the suicides,
cross-nailed, sea-gagged,
the Roman mobs,
the candy-chewing masses,
three days a week to bless
even myself, even you,
the whole unshaven world
with my astonishing purity —
adult happiness! adult sorrow!

Nick of the lost cedars, of the long silences,
of the translated Khayyám in the darkened window,
press your heated razor to the vein!

Ladders

I fished the way Frost farmed,
half-assed, and for the myth
the poems require. Why lie
about it? The performance
of any clown uses makeup
that the dark wipes off.

It's dark now. Frost mounts his ladder
to the only harvest he knew was his,
and I grip the iron rungs to a wharf
where no one walks. Why lie about it?

The skin of the apple is as cold
as the scales of the salmon
no matter the warm breath
of the taker. Here's a black rung
in the long, black ladder.
Do what the poets do, beyond pretense.
Press your body to something solid
and breathe harder.

Poets

*"Love's doorway to life
Is the same doorway everywhere."*
— Patrick Kavanaugh

The blood of the sockeye in the wood
the layers of warba dust on the knob
the nets heaped outside, inside the dead
fish laid stiff on the daily paper:
the door should have been too heavy
to open. The weight of the mud
at the steps, the wasps in their
angry suns at the sill, the rain
shoving its soaked body against
every human push.

But the door needed no kicking.
Our mother walked through it five times
and only one of us couldn't pass through
(he found another doorway, and somewhere
with our father he's calmly wiping
the smudge of the news of the world
off the bodies of the salmon
so they can taste the tides again). And me?
I took that knob into my touch
as if it were a woman's hand
and stepped into the blackberry musk
and drifted at the mouth of the river.

But I left the door open.
Your eyes, these words, are frame.
And there's no single direction.
Coming and going all our lives
we are love, we are memory,
we are the smoke off peat and cedar
rising from a stranger's chimney.

For Edward Thomas and David O'Meara

The rain falls in Oxfordshire
before the war and the barbed hooks
dropped in the fledglings' throats
to strangle song, and falls in Gwang-ju
on exiled Canadians teaching
the one world the one tune
to finance new laments
for a northern land, and falls here
but containing where else it falls,
rusting the Roman's breastplate,
sliding the great beasts downriver
to the millennial grave, glistening
the skin of the ripe cherries
and the flesh of the first girl
I ever kissed who reaches for them,
desire and the locus of desire,
nothing ever forgotten in this sound,
I can hear my father's breath,
Thomas whispering to Frost
across a stile, my friend mouthing
softly a Korean line. And now I think
the past is like a rain we walk in
but do not feel, just faintly hear,
the lips of the dead at my new son's ear,
saying "yours is the English daybreak
and the Asian dusk to wear
and all live voices at the bone."
But I can only guess at the telling.
It is what my father would say,
and the dead poet and the distant friend.
All the shattered syllables, all the rain.

Classic

Reading *Moby Dick* again, but landlocked,
the Rockies fast to one side, the prairies
loose to the other, and I alone in the house
to tell thee. A mighty book, writes Melville,
depends upon a mighty theme.

The cheap binding of my copy comes apart,
I see the glue, the pages flake away
with every turn, like delicate fillets
of whitefish. I have dropped
the chapter "Stubb's Supper" on the bus
and, with pathetic wit, remaindered a whole chunk
of blubbery prose on a table at Starbucks.
Soon I'll have left only the final italics.
If I could, I'd read them in the cabin
of my father's boat (long since firewood,
and my father ash) by the burning oil
of Leviathan.

I think the author meant us all
to lose our flesh and walk the earth
on pegs of what we kill and what
kills us. His book is a shrieking gull
whose wings keep tearing from my clutch.

When I am down to the last word
I will thrust my hand through the grass
into the stars and wave without surrender
that my children will mark the place
and cry the tears that scald pain,
their ships, their houses, their limbs,
fast to the loose weight of life.

Conception

On the tracks, like Colville's horse,
I faced my life. But my life
was stationary and I stood still
and the open country was the city:
car lots, coffee shops, corners hung
in breath and fumes.
Over these tracks I'd gone
a thousand times
to work, to friends,
and I had never stopped.

Today I stopped.
A heavy morning, the sun
a stray dog's blinded eye,
the wind in frozen scarves.

Head on, my life waited,
snake-still, poised to move
or not to move, its cold brow,
yellow peer, and history
of miles.

Slowly,
the blood-throb in the rails
the shiver in the earth
the hoof-beats in the temples
the sloughed skin of distance.

Slowly,
the planet in cloud
like the mind of the dog
in the milk of its eye.

But I was still.

Suddenly,
on the tracks, like Colville's horse,
I tore the bit
from the foaming moment of my will.

Young Men Fall in Love With Their Misery, Those Older Know It's Cold

Ten years since the slime of the living salmon
unctioned my hands. Starlight,
when last did I feel you? Blue heron,
how long since my eyesight frayed
at your wings' soaked coronas?

My children weren't made,
my father still breathed, I had,
like the day and the night,
everything to gain, everything to lose,
I had the moon without craters,
I had the shock of the schools
charging their valves at my wrists.

It is too easy for the spirit
to settle like a stump in the blood.
The charge took years to spark,
the spark years to flame,
the flame years to burn.

Can you hear the gills working
to let the black through the worlds?

Bloodchains, firecuffs. . .
Where I was, I'm still there.
This slime on my hands?
Birthwater.

Trainyards

I wrote my wife before she was my wife
and the letters went to a little apartment
at the edge of the trainyards, beside
a car-wrecker's and a plastic recycling
plant. At night, in bed, she would hear
the boxcars coupling and the engines
of the long freights hissing and sparking.
Her body, my letters, and the winter moon
were all that landscape knew of white;
even the snow was a charcoal sketch of snow.

She was lonely for my words before my body
so I put them down like kisses on the page.
In the mornings, she would cross the yards
to post her kissed replies, the engines
and the boxcars quiet, the new-
fallen snow titled "Woman as Swan
Crossing a Water of Ashes." It
was illegal and dangerous to be there.
But who could ever criticize
her beautiful trespasses?

Now the engines mourn her absence.
They are sad, hopelessly locked in their one line
into the city in which she has gone.
How I have come to pity them
the loss of her warm passage.

So sullenly they rest there, tortured
by the distant sparking of our bodies
through the hushed, mid-winter nights.

For Your Birthday

I would give you five minutes
of my childhood's summer dusks
for in those warm cocoons
grew all that is best
in me, praise and repose,
the praise in repose,
but I would give it
as it falls, alive, and
not as the fine dust of memory.

The moon widens over the river,
a spooked mare's eye,
and the river tenses its reins
to hold the sky in place.
Danger. But no one
with a heart is afraid.

The crickets sing for all five minutes,
or perhaps that's just an unoiled bike chain
squeaking the cherished mile
from the kitchen porch
to the rotted boatworks
in the marsh?

The whole way along the bank
over-ripe blackberries drop,
signets of August francing
Royal decrees.
But on a driftwood stump,
a blue heron stands like a pageboy
grown shabby in a court
where the ruling family
is so secure
they never have to issue orders.
Majesty, and majesty of languor,
in a dozen revolutions of the wheels.

Before the marsh of rushes, slanting
away level as a crewcut to the sloughs,
I stop to pick up the shed skin
of a garter snake. But this isn't memory,
I'm not a boy, and the best
of what I am, you have sprung
from its cocoon.

Here. Take this sheath
of rebirth in your hands.
My skin has written
on it "Yours"
a million times.
I travel now in praise
as a man travels whose life
owes its life to another.
The rust of memory is oiled
as the mare's eye shuts.
Peace. Now, silently,
the cherished distance to your touch.

Argument

Her face broke into one
of the many thousand
of rain-smeared
childhood windows
I stared through
at a landscape
of images bleeding
from the frames,
the splay of masts
in the harbour,
the black lab
blowing past
like a toddler's
soggy charcoal drawing,
the puddles darkening
to bruises
on the pavement,
the telephone lines
hung with the tears
of girls explaining to girls
that their boyfriends
just broke up with them.

The bones of my face
as I looked in her eyes
could not readjust.
What I saw
behind the blur
my hard words
had made
was colder, truer:
our children
aged, hurting,
tossing the last dirt
on my mouth.

Oh driver, your fleshless hands
on the wheel, turn the bus
so the window strikes the sun
and the child sees
only the gulls rising
from the dark fields
as my hands must
to touch the present moment
and her skin
with reconciling tenderness.

Rain on Sunday Afternoon

How many hours like this, yet not
like this, in our life of hours?
Heartbeat-of-a-bird quiet, silence
on the other side of silence.
Even the drips
off the eavestroughs
a part of the sheltering flock.

My book looms and fades,
a curious fish rising
to surface shadows and sinking
back. My head nestles
and snaps, then nestles again.

From somewhere in the notes
of rain, human notes proceed.
The neighbour-girl
at her piano, practising.
Something classical and yearning
though the girl is too young
to know how she supplements
the slow day's slippery losses
and subtle aches — what distance
between the fingers and the heart!

Half-asleep, I let the book fall
at last, and half-hear the music
through the thin, blurred pane,
the air outside gently broken
into beads of darker glass. All
is suddenly older than ourselves,
the book penned by one who's dead,
the song composed by one who's gone,
and the rain the same rain
that fell as they created
a semblance of what they heard
on the other side of it.

What a distance we travel
between our days and our life!

When, finally, the phone rings
and jolts me awake, and when I answer
and the mother of the girl-next-door
asks to speak with my wife
who's not here, and when from behind
the soft voice of this woman, our neighbour,
her daughter's piano-playing comes through,
and briefly I can hear
the two renditions, one no more and
no less an echo of the other, then
I know the bone-deep timbre
of the plunging hour
of every afternoon,
the other side of which
is always the heart's sure advance
toward yearning.

The Stern-End

I seek always the stern-end
of moments, occasions, inevitably
retire to the back porch
at house parties and find
the one star whose solitude
is greater, because older,
than my own, stay
to the very end of the credits
and as the wimpled plush
closes slow as a wave
cannot think but the world
is harsh and far from me
and I must walk into it
changed, though no one sees,
and polish my heart's blood
more at dusk than dawn,
the grit in the wake
of day grinding out
the deeper memory.

It is the bounty
of looking behind the world
that I have claimed
for my birthright
seeing the roe into fry
into the chainmail fist
slapped on the waters
and the scab mottling
the stilled scales
and the roe firing
in the cast of decay.

Not the scar in relation to the wound
but the healed-over flesh.
Not the smile in relation to the joy
but the wholeness of the life.

And language, the stern-end

of thought, feeling; inevitably
we come to it, and hang
over the flow, our reflections,
speaking little echoes from
parted mouths. Alone
on porches, in theatres,
over the sun's bloodying
of the water, ourselves
becoming the end of the poem.

ACKNOWLEDGEMENTS

"Pennies on the Sidewalk" was a finalist for the 2001 Bridport Prize and appeared in *The Bridport Prize Anthology* (Sansom & Company, Bristol, England).

"Old Trucks" and "Rain on Sunday Afternoon" appeared in *Arc*.

"The Great War" and "Dead Whale on the Ferry Causeway" appeared in *The Fiddlehead*.

"Owl Pellet" appeared in *The Malahat Review*.

"Grade One," "Paris, Youth, Springtime", and "Where the River Meets the Ocean" appeared in *Queen's Quarterly*.

Tim Bowling was born in Vancouver and raised in the nearby town of Ladner. He is the author of five previous collections of poetry and two novels. His most recent books are the novel *The Paperboy's Winter* (Penguin, 2003), and *The Witness Ghost* (Nightwood, 2003) which was short-listed for the Governor General's Award for Poetry. Bowling's poetry has garnered many prizes, including the Petra Kenney International Poetry Prize and the Canadian Authors Association Award for Poetry. Tim Bowling is editor of *Where the Words Come From: Canadian Poets in Conversation* (Nightwood, 2002). He lives in Edmonton.